# One-Minute
# SUCCESS
# SECRETS
## for Women

## Gail M. Hayes

D1048133

HARVEST HOUSE PUBLISHERS
EUGENE, OREGON

*Cover by Koechel Peterson & Associates, Inc., Minneapolis, Minnesota*

Published in association with the literary agency of The Steve Laube Agency, LLC, 5025 N. Central Ave., #635, Phoenix, Arizona, 85012.

**ONE-MINUTE SUCCESS SECRETS FOR WOMEN**
Copyright © 2012 by Gail M. Hayes
Published by Harvest House Publishers
Eugene, Oregon 97402
www.harvesthousepublishers.com
ISBN 978-0-7369-4938-5 (pbk.)
ISBN 978-0-7369-4939-2 (eBook)

**Printed in the United States of America**

13 14 15 16 17 18 19 / BP-KBD / 10 9 8 7 6 5 4 3 2

*To Mama T*
*Who took one minute to speak my name*
*and change my life*

# Introduction

*I*n one minute, your life can change dramatically. A storm ravages your neighborhood. Your boss looks at you sadly and says, "I'm sorry, but this just isn't working out." Your doctor calls you in to discuss that lump you hoped was benign. Your car rams into a guardrail…all in one minute. But good things can happen in that same minute too. A phone call comes from an old friend. An unexpected bonus arrives. A new job offer comes. A new love appears…all in one minute.

This book is for the woman who believes in the power of one minute. By taking the time to read one inspirational thought each day, you commit to activating change in your life. That change won't happen overnight, though. It takes steady, consistent progress toward a goal—a refusal to quit and a determination to keep going. That's a choice you have to keep making every minute of the day!

In this book are more than 100 tips and inspiring thoughts for your daily journey. They'll only take you one minute to read and digest, but they'll stick with you throughout the day, giving you the drive, energy, and encouragement you need to succeed! By the end, you'll have learned that success is no secret. It's just living life fully...one minute at a time!

# One Minute

*Study this Book of Instruction continually.*
*Meditate on it day and night so you will be sure to*
*obey everything written in it. Only then will you prosper*
*and succeed in all you do.*

JOSHUA 1:8

Take one minute and stand at the doorway marked *success*. You see it, don't you? It's the one with the star over your name printed on it. You want to push open the door to success, but you must be willing to work for that privilege. You must be willing to be patient, because the door might not open quickly. And you'll have to earn the right to push the door open. Success might come to those who abuse it, ignore it, devalue it, or dismiss it, but that's not the kind of success *you* want. Once you have it, you'll use it to help out your sisters and bring glory to God! If you take one minute to seek success with a heart filled with compassion, integrity, honesty, focus, and trustworthiness, that star will be yours!

# Three Things

*No, dear brothers and sisters, I have not achieved it,
but I focus on this one thing: Forgetting the past and
looking forward to what lies ahead, I press on to reach the
end of the race and receive the heavenly prize for which
God, through Christ Jesus, is calling us.*

PHILIPPIANS 3:13

There are three things you must do in this season of your life if you want to step into the blessings that await you.

You must be *free!*

You must be *fearless!*

You must be *fabulous!*

You must be free enough to experience new things in new ways. What worked yesterday will not work today. Tools you used on yesterday's projects will not work with today's ventures. The only way to access today's success is to upgrade your method of operation and your way of thinking. Read new books. Talk with new people who are further down the path than you are. Fears you once avoided you must now face. You must not allow those fears to keep you chained in doubt's dark shadows as your dreams pass you by. Unashamedly pursue your dreams. This year choose to be free, fearless, and fabulous. It's the only way to go!

# The Sound

*Those who live at the ends of the earth stand in awe of*
*your wonders. From where the sun rises to where it sets,*
*you inspire shouts of joy.*

PSALM 65:8

*P*assion can invite you to new places. Passion can envelope you and make you see things you've never seen. Passion can overtake you and give you wings. But how will you recognize it? What does it look like? How does it sound?

Is it like the rain, calming and exciting you at the same time? Does it drown out the clanging sounds of trouble? When it falls on your life's rooftop, it might create a space that allows you to hear destiny whisper your name. Once you hear that voice, you will never be the same. You can then hear above life's noises and recognize the still, small voice that allows power to flow into your life like a rushing, mighty river overflowing its banks.

Is it like fire? Fire crackles. Fire burns. Fire creates heat and causes the atmosphere to change with such force that it sometimes causes human emotions to surge, uncontrolled. It causes everything in its path to bow or be destroyed. All negative influences must stop in its path. Toxic thoughts, venomous plots, envious glances, and jealous whispers cease because they cannot prosper in the path of destiny ignited by passion's fire.

So, what does inspiration look like to you?

# Others

*But in that coming day no weapon turned
against you will succeed. You will silence every
voice raised up to accuse you.*

ISAIAH 54:17

When others persecute you, remember that they don't know you so they can't possibly see the real you. When others hate you, remember that they haven't taken the time to see you as you really are. When others abuse you, remember that they don't know your purpose because they did not create you. When others talk negatively about you, remember that they really have nothing to talk about. Talking about others is all they do! Their words have no real impact upon you or your life. When others develop plots or schemes against you, remember that their plans cannot prosper and their weapons will not work when the attack comes. So put them on notice! Do not stand still and allow their behavior to change you.

# True Wisdom

*Wisdom is more precious than rubies; nothing you
desire can compare with her.*

PROVERBS 3:15

True wisdom knows when to speak and when to keep silent. Wisdom knows that if you speak before you understand a situation, insight can escape through the window that ignorance has opened prematurely. Wisdom knows when to move and when to stand still. It knows that if you move in the wrong direction or if you procrastinate, all you've worked for can disappear in an instant. Dreams and plans mean nothing if arrogance litters your path. Wisdom lets you know when to seize the moment and when to allow the moment to capture you. It knows when to move and then allows you to grasp what belongs to you. Wisdom knows that once it captures you, you can ride upon its magnificent wind without fear.

# Appreciation

*Let your roots grow down into him, and let your*
*lives be built on him. Then your faith will grow*
*strong in the truth you were taught, and you*
*will overflow with thankfulness.*

COLOSSIANS 2:7

It is not often someone comes into your life with no expectations except to love you. If you forget, they forgive. If you ignore them, they endure. If you don't show up, they understand. If you put them on hold, they watch the blinking light. If you break a promise, they still see the good in you. If you make it rain, they pull out the umbrella with a smile. They want what's best for you more than you want it for yourself. They hold up a mirror and allow you to see your greatness reflected there. They put you first. They feel what you feel, even when you are apart. They celebrate you even when the crowd stops applauding you. They redirect their sunlight to shine on you and keep you warm when failure's chilly winds try to blast you from destiny's pathway. They believe in you when no one else does. But time's ocean has a way of washing these beautiful things away. When someone like this comes into your life, don't let them leave with the tide and be lost forever with the next passing wave. You will then pay a heavy price, purchased with unappreciation's currency.

# Illegal Aliens

*And now, dear brothers and sisters, one final thing. Fix*
*your thoughts on what is true, and honorable, and right,*
*and pure, and lovely, and admirable. Think about things*
*that are excellent and worthy of praise.*

PHILIPPIANS 4:8

Give anger his pink slip because he lost his job today. Terminate stress because his assignment is finished! Give despair leave to go because hope has replaced him! Show negative conversation the door! He is no longer welcome. All he will do is offer excuses and blame others for his behavior. Discouragement cannot remain unless you give him space. Eject him from that comfortable chair and put him out! And tell him to take his chair with him. You do not want any residue from his visit left in your atmosphere. Close your borders to negative whispers. They are toxic and they destroy destiny! They leave their scum on everything they touch. It's time to clean out and deodorize your camp. It's time to do you in a new way. You don't have time for negative weight! It's time for you to live free and rid your kingdom of everything that doesn't push you forward!

# A Good Fight

*Be courageous! Let us fight bravely for our people and the cities of our God.*

2 SAMUEL 10:12

You learn from your youth that a battle rages between good and evil. You make daily decisions to march with the evil or to take a city with the good. Both commanders watch from their command posts, hoping you will fight for their cause.

You have the wonder of love and power of choice working for you. If you deal in dark whispers or develop secret plots against the innocent, then you use your gifts to increase the darkness. If you serve others with love, acceptance, and honor, then you fight for good. Which army do you serve? Remember that someone is desperate for the good you bring to the table. Your light can illuminate their darkest hour. So today, make a decision to serve the army of light and give the army of darkness what they deserve…a good fight they can never win!

# Boundaries

*Your own ears will hear him. Right behind*
*you a voice will say, "This is the way you should go,"*
*whether to the right or to the left.*

ISAIAH 30:21

Setting boundaries is serious business. When something or someone is not serving you well (especially when they can do better), then it is okay to set new boundaries. You don't need to accept mediocrity or leftovers. The only way you can bring honor to relationships is by establishing appropriate boundaries. Once you understand the power of being able to say no, you will see that holding your own is more than possible.

Remember this: even if a situation is critical, it's not necessarily your crisis. Just because something is important to others doesn't mean that it is your mission. Just because something is exciting to others doesn't mean that you need to sit and partake. Something that has appeal to others doesn't have to bring you joy. Something may appear to be essential to others but it could be a waste of your time if it's not your life's mission. Remember that it is within the realm of your power to set boundaries. Without them, your territory would become a barren land overrun by ruthless invaders.

# Friends

*There is no greater love than to lay down
one's life for one's friends.*

JOHN 15:13

It's great to have friends who encourage you and let you know when you're on the right path. They tell you the truth even when you don't want to hear it. They hold up your arms during the battle. They hold your shield so you can draw your sword. They run with you to meet the enemy. They share in the spoils of war as you celebrate victory. They stand with you to face defeat.

When facing monumental changes, these warriors still love you. They do not abandon you in your time of need. They help you stand when all you want to do is sit. They help you fight when all you want to do is give up. They help you win when you feel like you are losing your mind. And when you're just about to despair, these warriors remind you that you still have work to do. Treasure them. Cherish them. And keep them close.

# The Battle

*Control your temper, for anger labels you a fool.*
ECCLESIASTES 7:9

*A*nger battled peace today. When anger showed up, it brought with it brutal, pounding waves. Did the waves win the day? No, because the wind and water pounded walls of personal resistance to no avail. You stood against these attacks and survived like a seasoned warrior.

These forces were unsuccessful in their bid to defeat you and bring you down. They did not transform your joy into sorrow. They did not move mountains to expose hideous valleys of separation. They did not destroy bridges connecting the cities where love, hope, peace, and all things lovely dwell.

You know why? Because God built those bridges, and He maintains your peace against the waves of anger and bitterness!

# The Coulda, Shoulda, Woulda Blues

*Fear not; you will no longer live in shame.*
*Don't be afraid; there is no more disgrace for you.*
*You will no longer remember the shame of your youth*
*and the sorrows of widowhood.*

ISAIAH 54:4

Ever wondered why so many people come to the end of life and have the "coulda, shoulda, woulda" blues? They coulda chosen to serve others but they were building up treasure for themselves instead. They shoulda helped someone out of trouble but they were too busy with their own problems. They woulda done something different but they never risked that leap of faith.

Why do you think they caught the blues? It's because they were scared. Fear of commitment, fear of success, fear of trusting others, fear of truly living, fear of happiness, fear of intimacy, fear of love, fear of doing, being, holding, and experiencing something great.

These things make life worth living, so don't come to the end of life and say you coulda had love but you never loved back, you shoulda connected but you didn't have time, and you woulda been happy but you never took a chance. Kick coulda, shoulda, woulda to the curb and experience life without regrets!

# Relationships

*A friend is always loyal, and a brother is born to help in time of need.*

PROVERBS 17:17

People give care and attention to those who have meaning or hold importance to them. That's how you want to be treated, right? With care and attention?

So how do you treat others in your relationships? Do you nurture others? Or do you disregard their feelings and make them feel unimportant? No one should settle for scraps from your table, and if you ask someone to you may lose a friendship and never recover what you lost. If you want a relationship, cherish it. Cherish the people in your life. Relationships take work and a commitment of time and energy. Are you willing to work for what you want?

# Gifts

*The human body has many parts, but the many parts make up one whole body. So it is with the body of Christ.*

1 Corinthians 12:12

Sure, you have gifts. Everyone does. A gift for leadership, for discernment, for nurturing, for teaching, for listening. But how will you use the gifts you've been given?

Remember that you can't use your gifts in isolation. You must develop them in communion with others, sharing one another's talents and abilities and learning from others' experiences. As you do so, serve others without regret. Remember that you will never sit with the great if you are not grateful. You will never sit with the powerful if you are not willing to serve others. Listen to wisdom. Listen to those experienced in battle. And then share your gifts freely, because gifts are meant to be given away.

# There Will Never Be Another

*Don't brag about tomorrow, since you don't know what the day will bring.*

PROVERBS 27:1

There will never be another day like today. There will never be a sunrise painted like the one you saw this morning. The birds will never sing their song the same way they did today.

And there will never be another time like now. This is a time of movement. This is a time of recapturing the dreams you lost yesterday when procrastination ruled. You cannot let him win today! You will never be able to recapture this day or the opportunities offered in this moment. You will never be as ready as you are today.

Tomorrow's effort cannot handle today's weight. So live with passion today. Love like it's the last time you'll be able to love, to embrace, to touch, and to feel. Take hold of this moment with both hands and seize the opportunities that will fade away when the sun sets. Don't allow fear to keep you from finishing a task, hugging a friend, or taking the next step on your journey. There will never be another moment like today.

# Older and Wiser

*Wisdom belongs to the aged, and understanding to the old.*
JOB 12:12

Being an older woman has its advantages. You no longer need permission to do what you want, when you want, how you want, with anyone you want. You understand the value of wisely using your gifts, and you know what can happen when you don't use them the way God intended. You understand the negative impact of inactivity and procrastination. You understand honor and know that when you give it freely, it comes back to you. You've made your mistakes and learned from them, and your experience helps you make better decisions now. And best of all, you can pass that wisdom along to your younger sisters. You can give them the benefit of that experience and teach them to live a life without regrets!

# Valuable

*Who can find a virtuous and capable wife?*
*She is more precious than rubies.*

PROVERBS 31:10

iamonds, rubies, pearls, sapphires, and emeralds. Just the names of these jewels send shivers down a girl's spine. Gold and silver settings hold our jewels and catch the sun's light while making many a girl giggle with joy. These jewels don't have to search for customers. They don't have to advertise themselves and beg you to take a closer look. Customers seek them out, looking for the perfect gem.

Are you "more precious than rubies" in your relationships? Do your friends, relatives, and coworkers understand your value? Do they appreciate your time? Do they honor what you bring into their lives? Do they realize that you paint their world with the color of your life in ways that others can't?

You should not have to beg anyone to spend time with you, love you, or be kind to you. If you're not valued in your current relationships, move on, girl! Because you're more valuable than diamonds, rubies, pearls, sapphires, or emeralds.

# Doubt

*Then Jesus told him, "I tell you the truth, if you have faith
and don't doubt, you can do things like this and much
more. You can even say to this mountain, 'May you be
lifted up and thrown into the sea,' and it will happen."*

MATTHEW 21:21

If you are in doubt about your future, then doubt will
plague your destiny. Doubt will walk with you. Doubt
will talk with you. Doubt will embrace you. Doubt will hold
your dreams captive. He will lock them in fear's dark dun-
geon and then erase them from your memory bank. Then he
will stand in your face and rip the breath from your doubting
lungs. He will joyfully rip the life out of you if you allow him!

Doubt feeds on your fear. If you are in doubt about your
power, then doubt will overpower you. Doubt will take control over your life. Doubt will knock you down as you stand
on your tiptoes trying to reach your goals. Doubt will cling
to you, your dance partner for life. If you doubt that you are
valuable, then doubt will stand as a witness that you hold
no value.

Don't give your destiny away to doubt. Believe! With
faith, you can move mountains into the sea.

# Timing Is Everything

*For everything there is a season, a time for*
*every activity under heaven.*

ECCLESIASTES 3:1

*T*iming is everything. When you pray for a situation and things don't go the way you want them to, it doesn't mean the answer is no. It may just mean that the timing is not right for what you want or that things are not yet in place for your perfect view. Maybe you can't see clearly yet.

Having a perfect view is a wondrous gift and is reserved for those willing to wait until the right time. When the time is right, things fall into place. When the time is right, your dreams can become reality. When the time is right, your hard work will pay off. When the time is right, miracles really can happen. When the time is right, love will come. When the time is right, mysteries you've pondered become a reality. When the time is right, success will embrace you and you will never be the same. Timing is everything...so wait for the view!

# Downpour

*All who are victorious will inherit all these blessings, and*
*I will be their God, and they will be my children.*

REVELATION 21:7

Remember when you were a child, dancing outside during a rainstorm? Do you remember how you loved the smell and feel of the rain? Well, it's raining wherever you are if you believe in blessings. You must first believe that you are standing in a place that is ripe for blessing. Today is a day of blessing, and you can either experience them as they come to you or ignore them. It's your choice, and choice is a powerful force. It can lead you down the road to failure or catapult you to destiny. It can cause you to soar upon the winds of change or crawl on the broken glass of stagnation.

Blessings await you. Blessings are calling your name. Blessings are groaning with the weight of creation because they look for places to dwell. Couldn't you use some blessings right about now? They're on their way, so you can run to meet them! Ready or no...there they come! Don't just stand there! Get outside and dance in that heavenly rain!

# Breakthrough

*For every child of God defeats this evil world, and we
achieve this victory through our faith.*

1 JOHN 5:4

Have you ever been so frustrated that you felt like you couldn't go on? Have you longed for a change but couldn't see a clear path to another destination? Have you ever felt like nothing you touched prospered, nothing you did could change your situation, and nothing you said mattered? Are you sick and tired of being sick and tired?

If you are ready for something new and something different, then it's time for a break. Close your eyes and see yourself leaping over stumbling blocks. Close your eyes and see yourself moving mountains. Close your eyes and envision yourself kicking over obstacles. Sure, they'll still be there when you open your eyes, but you'll have the energy and the drive to make that restful vision a reality! Come on, girl—it's time for a breakthrough!

# Tomorrow

*I know all the things you do, and I have opened a
door for you that no one can close.*

REVELATION 3:8

As you stand at the door leading to tomorrow, remember that not everyone will have the opportunity to view the open door. The doorway is not visible to all your sisters. Frustration blinds the eyes of those who hold bitterness close and those who bask in envy's murky presence. Not everyone will get to experience the sights and sounds of tomorrow. The sights and sounds of tomorrow are reserved for those who keep looking ahead. You cannot see into tomorrow if you refuse to let go of the past. Not everyone will be able to step into the winds of change and have the opportunity to make a difference. The path before you leads to destiny. Will you answer destiny's call or listen to the sorrowful voices of the past? If you want to make a difference... let go!

# Golden Rule

*Do to others whatever you would like them to do to you.*
*This is the essence of all that is taught in the law and the*
*prophets.*

MATTHEW 7:12

❧

It is such a gift to know that people love you. It is such a gift to have them acknowledge you in the way you need to be acknowledged, to let you know that what you do and what you say is important to them. It means so much to have them ask about your day, to thank you when you've done something for them, and to give little mementos of affection just because they know that they please you and you love those things.

Those nuggets are like mini chests overflowing with treasures. So are you giving these treasures as well as receiving them? If not, take a look at your life. Help others fill their chests with gifts. You never know how a kind word or gesture will lift up your sister in need!

# When You Move Forward

*I don't mean to say that I have already achieved
these things or that I have already reached perfection.
But I press on to possess that perfection for which
Christ Jesus first possessed me.*

PHILIPPIANS 3:12

*Y*ou want to move forward, but what happens when
you look back? What happens when you take your
eyes off your designated path?

You miss details. You miss opportunities. You miss obstacles ahead of you and run into boulders that block your way.
You race over landmarks needed for success in your journey.

You must look ahead if you want success. You have to
decide to look forward to new opportunities, to try new
things without fear, to be unafraid of new relationships, to
seize the moments that call your name, and to walk in the
fullness of your gifts because it truly does not serve you or
others to minimize yourself. Decide that you will no longer
be intimidated by your potential. So keep moving forward
and watch as greatness overtakes you!

# Don't Get Angry...
# Get Queenly!

*Better to be patient than powerful; better to have
self-control than to conquer a city.*

PROVERBS 16:32

Whenever anger wants to dance with you, remember you wear a crown and you don't dance with strangers. Whenever frustration begs to whisper in your ear, remember that he cannot come into your presence unless summoned. Whenever fear decides to walk in your park, have him escorted back into the wilderness. He is trespassing and is no longer welcome. Whenever sorrow requests an audience, tell joy, gladness, and happiness to bar him from coming into the throne room of your life. Jealousy, strife, envy, gossip, and all their companions stand waiting to gain access to royalty. Ignore their decrees. They have no place in the realm of the queenly. It's up to you. You can allow them into your presence or not. It's time to reign in your domain!

# Powerful One

*You guide me with your counsel, leading
me to a glorious destiny.*

PSALM 73:24

❧

ou are the daughter of the King, and it's time for you to discover the majesty of your royal existence! It's time for you to embrace the beauty of your wonderful identity. It's time for you to dance in the light of your purpose and to embrace your magnificent destiny. It's time to accept yourself for who you are and stand in the splendid radiance of your destiny. It's time to touch others with your unique light, your singular style, and your matchless ability to change the world around you. It's time for you to shatter evil by standing for good, even when it's not the popular thing to do. It's time for you to speak words that bring healing, give smiles that bring joy, and give hugs that conquer fear!

# Run!

*We can rejoice, too, when we run into problems and trials,
for we know that they help us develop endurance. And
endurance develops strength of character, and character
strengthens our confident hope of salvation.*

ROMANS 5:3-4

Run! Run to face challenges. Sure, it takes courage, but courage is the drink of champions. Stand at his fountain, fill your cup, and run! Run to face the trials that others say you cannot overcome. Run to overtake the winds of new life, new adventures, and undiscovered joy.

And remember that most voices speak discouragement when faced with obstacles. They will never see mountaintops. They will never view the richness that waits on the other side of the mountain. Don't let those voices bring you down, because once you're running it's only a matter of time before you can fly…without wings!

# Live the Impossible

*Never let loyalty and kindness leave you!*
*Tie them around your neck as a reminder.*
*Write them deep within your heart.*

PROVERBS 3:3

Writing is healing. When you are lonely, you can string your painful thoughts into pearls of joy. When you are angry, you can transform your rage into lyrical images. When you lack inspiration in your life, you can create a fire not easily extinguished. When you lose your faith, you can create an atmosphere ripe for miracles. And when you lack purpose, you can hatch a plan.

The words you pen set sail across tribulation's seas and then anchor you on the other side of trouble. Writing creates new and different ways of thinking. It releases you into new worlds where you can do the impossible. It allows you to create, enjoy, dream, and live!

# There Are Giants in the Land

*David asked the soldiers standing nearby, "...Who is this pagan Philistine anyway, that he is allowed to defy the armies of the living God?"*

1 SAMUEL 17:26

There are giants in the land and there is something you should know about them. Take a closer look and you can see them as they really are. Whether you choose to believe it, feel it, see it or experience it...they fear you! When you look at them through the lens of courage, they shrink. You can then see that they are spineless. They are weak. They have no stature. Their words have no meaning. Their breathing is shallow because they cannot survive in your atmosphere!

When you examine them, you can see that they are hills, not mountains. They are shallow valleys, not deep crevasses. They are babbling brooks, not oceans. They are infants, not warriors. So why should you fear them? Why should you hesitate to take your land?

Those giants quake, shake, tremble, and shrink in the presence of the King—and you, His daughter! Don't let the giants fool you. They fear you!

# Promises

*The one who...speaks the truth from their heart,
whose tongue utters no slander...and casts no slur on
others...who keeps an oath even when it hurts, and does
not change their mind...whoever does these
things will never be shaken.*

PSALM 15:2-5

*Y*our promises carry your signature. They carry your very character! Whenever you make a promise, consider the weight of your words. Those words are building blocks of either faith or frustration, courage or fear, love or hate, life or death.

What are you building with your words? Are you establishing trust? Are you speaking truth and proclaiming honor with every breath? When you make a promise, can the listener have confidence that you'll carry it out? Your character rides on your words. Do you honor and value them? Or do you fling honor into the cold ground of instability? Never forget it for an instant: Your words have weight.

# Victory

*For every child of God defeats this evil world,*
*and we achieve victory through our faith.*

1 John 5:4

 othing tastes as good as victory. Nothing smells as
 sweet as a mission accomplished. Nothing feels as
good as heaving a sigh of relief after completing a difficult
project and knowing it's done well. And there are few experiences that compare with looking through your rearview
mirror and seeing the obstacles you overcame on the road
to your destiny.

You accomplished this staying focused and believing that
victory was possible. You sensed that this was your moment
of destiny and that nothing and no one could stop you. So
enjoy your victory! Taste it, smell it, hear it, feel it! It was
bought with the sweat of your brow, the execution of your
plans, the belief in your heart, and a heavenly sacrifice more
awesome than you can describe.

# Step and Shake the Earth

*The LORD directs the steps of the godly. He delights
in every detail of their lives.*

PSALM 37:23

Girl, you shake the earth when you step! People move. Obstacles move. Your footsteps set things in motion. But this only happens when you move. You cannot allow fear to overtake you. You cannot allow procrastination to hold you. You cannot allow negative whispers to hinder you. You cannot allow people who try and block your way or sabotage you to stop you. As soon as you step, they will fall from your path. They cannot stand in the path of the righteous.

So take a step. Nothing can hold a bold stepper. Nothing can stop someone on a focused mission. Sure, life can set up obstacles. Life can cause delay. But these things cannot stop you unless you stop stepping. So keep it moving!

# Let Them Go

*For I am about to do something new. See, I have already begun! Do you not see it? I will make a pathway through the wilderness. I will create rivers in the dry wasteland.*

ISAIAH 43:19

It's hard to lose someone who has been close to you. It's challenging to see a friendship dissolve or to watch a relationship decay. Suffering a loss of connection can be heartbreaking. But there are times when you have to chart a path to another location and find a new destination. You have to move away—your journey is taking you to a place you hadn't expected. The season of connection may have expired and you have to make room for God to surprise you with new blessings.

This should be a time of rejoicing. Celebrate what you shared and all you've accomplished together. Celebrate the joyful times you'll always cherish. And then open your eyes to the ways God is already working in this new stage of your life!

# One of Those Days

*So be truly glad. There is wonderful joy ahead, even though you have to endure many trials for a little while.*

1 Peter 1:6

Have you ever had one of those days when everything seemed to fall apart? Where hostility reigned supreme as it strangled hope and inspiration? Where your best efforts seemed fruitless and unfinished products laughed at you from the shadows? Where harsh words stung your heart like porcupine quills? Where love evaporated in jealousy's desert heat?

Remember, even heroes experienced hostility, jealousy's sting, and laughter from those who hated them. The pain made them strong. The harsh winds strengthened them and gave them the ability to stand in the terrible rain of opposition. Endurance through the trials made them great!

# Explore

*So then, let us aim for harmony in the church and try to build each other up.*

ROMANS 14:19

Explore. Explore the unknown. Explore your feelings. Explore your intentions. Explore the love light in someone's eyes.

Explore why you haven't done what you know you need to do. Explore why you keep waiting on tomorrow instead of boldly facing *today*. Explore why you entertain complainers. Explore why you allow them to infect your atmosphere. Explore why you spend time with those who mean you no good. Explore why you don't spend time with those who do. Explore why you know that it's time to make changes but you hesitate.

Explore. Change direction. Kick fear aside and then explore that thing called joy, the freedom of accomplishment, and a newness of life the likes of which you have never experienced! Explore!

# Shameless

*To all who mourn in Israel, he will give a crown*
*of beauty for ashes, a joyous blessing instead of mourning,*
*festive praise instead of despair. In their righteousness,*
*they will be like great oaks that the LORD has*
*planted for his own glory.*

ISAIAH 61:3

*Y*ou are shameless! You are shamelessly beautiful. Shamelessly powerful. Shamelessly regal. Shamelessly wonderful. Shamelessly awesome.

Why can you live without shame? Because Christ paid a heavy price for you to know it, speak it, and live it. Christ ransomed you. He pulled back shame's dark curtain and ripped you from its tormenting embrace. He allowed you to feel love's tenderness, allowed you to experience the light of something shamelessly grand.

So now you can shamelessly chase your dreams. You can shamelessly love yourself so that you may shamelessly love others. You can shamelessly help those who have fallen to stand. You can shamelessly stop and dry the tears of those caught in the pit of shame-filled lives. When others look at you, you want them to see that there is no shame in you. You want them to see that you are living free and without shame because Christ died for you to be shamelessly you!

# Character

*If you are kind only to your friends, how are you different
from anyone else? Even pagans do that.*

MATTHEW 5:47

The true test of your character is not how you treat those who love you but rather how you treat those who hate you. There is no greatness in being kind to those who are kind to you. It takes little energy to connect with those who smile when they see you, who open the arms of friendship when they come into your presence. How do you react when people throw stones at you? Are you still able to pray for them? Love them as God's chosen children? Can you still take the time for someone who's an inconvenience? Who gets in the way of your success?

Today, extend a hand to an enemy. Say a prayer for them. Show the love of Christ through your character.

# The Right Fit

*He makes the whole body fit together perfectly.*
*As each part does its own special work, it helps the other*
*parts grow, so that the whole body is healthy and*
*growing and full of love.*

EPHESIANS 4:16

*Y*ou know how it feels when you find a pair of shoes
that fit? Or when you pull on a dress that shows off
the best you? You examine yourself in the mirror and grin,
because girl, you're looking good!

It's the same with discovering who you are and where
you fit. When you find the right job, the right church, the
right relationship, you know it's a good fit! Once you find
that place, you can do just about anything you decide to do.
You're in exactly the right place for God to use you and work
through you! And best of all, when you find a good fit you
can stand back and help a sister out! Help her find *her* perfect fit, and see how you can all work together!

45

# Unique

*But you are not like that, for you are a chosen people. You
are royal priests, a holy nation, God's very own possession.
As a result, you can show others the goodness of God, for he
called you out of the darkness into his wonderful light.*

1 PETER 2:9

Sure, you fit into a personality type. You like some of the
same things your friends do. But girl, did you know
that you are unique? God created you unlike anyone else
in the world. You can do things others cannot do. You can
say things others may not be able to say. And no one else on
earth is called to live out the mission and purpose that are
uniquely yours.

As you walk and talk, as you process information, and as
you connect with others, remember that no one else is quite
like you. You're not just another face in the crowd. You matter! And everyone around you matters too. Your friends, your
family, your coworkers—all of them are dearly loved and
uniquely created for their own special purpose.

# Dare

*For I can do everything through*
*Christ, who gives me strength.*

PHILIPPIANS 4:13

Today, dare to do something you've never done before. Dare to experience something you've always longed to try. Dare to stand in the face of adversity and laugh as fear tries to have his way with you. He can't win unless you give in. And girl, you've got so much to do that you can't allow him to stop you. Dare to believe that you are more powerful than you think and more awesome than you imagined. Dare to love more, do more, think more, say more, be more. Dare to be really happy. Dare to look forward—not back into a dismal past. If you have the courage to envision it, you can do it…if you dare.

# Not Everyone

*This is the day the LORD has made.*
*We will rejoice and be glad in it.*

PSALM 118:24

Not everyone will wake up this morning and have the opportunity to enjoy the day. Not everyone will be able to rise when the day begins. Not everyone will luxuriate in the sun's warmth or feel the breeze of newness that embraces the day. Not everyone will see the majesty of the night sky and breathe in the fiery beauty of the stars. Not everyone will have the opportunity to meet new people, create new relationships, or make their dreams and visions a reality. Not everyone will lift their head and smile at the challenges ahead.

You are not like everyone else. You have been given the gift of today. There is greatness in you and gratitude should be your middle name. So today arise and walk in His greatness and remember: Rejoice!

# Freedom

*Oh, give me back my joy again;*
*you have broken me—now let me rejoice.*

PSALM 51:8

Freedom isn't always free. It's hard to break away from the old attitudes and prejudices that have long held you captive. If jealousy has been your friend, then jealousy isn't going to just let you walk away. It will haunt you with its siren song and try to make you believe that it still has power over you. If you've danced in the dark with fear, then fear isn't going to quickly step aside and let you find another partner who will share the light. He will continue to cast his shadow over you for as long as you allow him to do so. If you've drunk from anger's cup, then anger isn't going to rejoice when you find another favorite beverage. He will continue to place his poisonous drops into your cup and smile as you sip.

This means that you will have to fight for your freedom! Are you willing to fight? Are you willing to see these attitudes fall and not pick them up again? Are you ready to be free?

# You Have Been Chosen

*For you are a holy people, who belong to the LORD your God. Of all the people on earth, the LORD your God has chosen you to be his own special treasure.*

DEUTERONOMY 7:6

You have been chosen to do great things:

- to live in this moment
- to touch others with the fire of your greatness
- to create newness
- to unchain minds held captive by toxic thoughts
- to do good and not evil
- to show others how to be loyal
- to help those in need
- to demonstrate the power of kindness
- to emit the fragrance of destiny to those lost in confusion's web
- to be the authentic, capable, beautiful, and powerful you!

None of this is easy, but you can do it because you know you're not alone. You've got some powerful backup! He chose you to do all these things and more. Never forget: you've been chosen!

# Honor

*He will set you high above all the other nations he has
made. Then you will receive praise, honor, and renown.
You will be a nation that is holy to the LORD your God,
just as he promised.*

DEUTERONOMY 26:19

When someone dishonors you, it doesn't make you dishonorable. When someone can't see your value, it simply means that they are ignorant. Don't give their opinion the time of day. They are blinded by jealousy's cataracts, by fear's fatal embrace, by the contaminated atmosphere of ignorance, and by the corrosion of their own dreams. Each time they dishonor you, they erode the beauty of a pure connection.

But have you ever thought that you may be the one needed to help them move to the next step in their journey? The one who can help them embrace their most passionate inner vision? Try not to get angry when they dishonor you. They are blind and caught in destruction's trap. They are waiting for someone bold enough, strong enough, and regal enough to speak a word of deliverance in their lives. Can you be that person today?

# Hurting People

*Give justice to the poor and the orphan; uphold
the rights of the oppressed and destitute.*

PSALM 82:3

You've heard it said that hurting people hurt people. Hurting people gossip about other people. Hurting people discourage other people. Hurting people betray other people. Hurting people destroy other people. Hurting people hate other people. Why? Because hurting people usually hate themselves. They are not whole. Discouragement and anguish have rained in their lives and they stood unprepared in the storm with broken umbrellas.

But you have an umbrella and a raincoat! You love life and enjoy living. You saw the storm coming and you prepared. You can't help but love people because whole people help other people. Whole people speak good words over other people. Whole people encourage other people. Whole people support other people. Whole people build up other people. Whole people love other people. Thank God that you are a whole person!

# There Is Nothing More Powerful

*I look up to the mountains—does my help
come from there? My help comes from the LORD,
who made heaven and earth!*

PSALM 121:1-2

There is nothing more powerful than a woman who understands that when things look down, she needs to look up. It takes strength to look up, especially if you've been unable to see the sky in your world because the fog of discontent clouds your vision. But now you know it's time to look up, and you must activate your strength in ways you've never had to do before. You must engage your back muscles. They lock into place and ready themselves to support your shoulders and neck. Then and only then can you tilt your head up. Your eyes can then see a new way of doing things, a new way of envisioning the future, a new way to perceive the possibilities that have been surrounding you all along.

Once you look up, you understand that success also means looking outside yourself to find answers to difficult questions and to find solutions to challenges that have long held your life captive. When you need help, lift your head. When you need counsel, lift your eyes. When you need clarity, lift your arms and hands upward and behold the miraculous!

# When Things Look Dark

*The night is almost gone; the day of salvation will soon be here. So remove your dark deeds like dirty clothes, and put on the shining armor of right living.*

ROMANS 13:12

Things look dark today. You feel oppressed by all the responsibilities that are crowding out your joy. But if you look closely, you will see that there is always a ray of light in the gloomiest of situations. There is always a glimmer of expectation, a spark of joy, a belief that something unexpected can still happen. There is always a twinkle of anticipation that causes the spirit to leap with unexpected hope.

It is a hope that cannot be deferred, a hope that cannot be extinguished by negative whispers, a hope that allows passion to have her way. That hope might be the smallest spark, but it can still illuminate the heart. That small spark causes those who are faint in heart to become the leaders who show others the way out of darkness. Look for that spark of hope today, no matter how dark things seem!

# New Every Morning

*The faithful love of the LORD never ends!*
*His mercies never cease. Great is his faithfulness;*
*his mercies begin afresh each morning.*

LAMENTATIONS 3:22-23

Every time you think you know everything about life, the Lord decides to teach you something new. This is no time to become apathetic or jaded! There's always a new discovery beyond the horizon—some new way of looking at life. That's why you should love getting up each morning. There is always a new day with a new beginning. You've never smelled the fragrance of that day or tasted the sweetness of new love before. So run to meet the day and experience the great possibilities that are wrapped up in the gift box of opportunity. This gift sits on the table of your morning and awaits your arrival. And guess what? No one can open it but you!

# Catch a Falling Star

*He counts the stars and calls them all by name.*

PSALM 147:4

*H*ave you ever tried to catch a falling star? Even if you were standing in the heavens, you couldn't do it. It just can't be done by mere mortals. Only God has the power to catch a star, or reverse the course of a comet!

And you know what? You're just like that star! Only God has the power to stop you in your tracks and reverse the course of your life. If anyone else tries to stop you, they can't do it! They can't stop you from succeeding. They can't stop you from moving. They can't stop you from loving, from giving, from living, from shining in the face of adversity, or from being you! The haters can't block your way. They can't stop you from doing what you do. So, shine on, girl, because there is only one force in the universe that can catch a star and He is not trying to stop you. He wants you to shine. He wants you to succeed. He wants you to be all He created you to be! So shine on, girl!

# Popcorn

*Give, and you will receive. Your gift will be returned to
you in full—pressed down, shaken together to make room
for more, running over, and poured into your lap. The
amount you give will determine the amount you get back.*

LUKE 6:38

Gifts are like popcorn. They start out as kernels, not
good for much but full of potential. But when you
apply a little heat, things pop! It's the same way with the
unique talents and abilities God has given you. When you
put the right energy behind your gifts, you cause things to
"pop" like you never dreamed possible.

In other words, it's okay to go after what you want. It's
okay to be successful. It's okay to live a life filled with marvelous wonder. It's okay to breathe, laugh, love, live, and
be totally you—with no excuses! Life is too short to sit and
wish things had turned out differently. If you want things to
be different, then you must do something differently! What
are you willing to risk in order to use your gifts the way God
intended? It's never too late to be happy. So start the "pop-
ping" and move! Turn up the heat and unashamedly use your
gifts. They were meant to be given away and shared—just
like a big bowl of popcorn!

# Three Things

*Praise his name with dancing, accompanied by*
*tambourine and harp.*

PSALM 149:3

There are three things you need today: love, laughter, and music.

When you love, hate has no space to occupy.

When you stand in the face of adversity and laugh, you triumph.

When you hear music, you can dance your way out of harm's embrace.

There is nothing you cannot accomplish today if you love, laugh, and stay in step with the music of your self-composed melody. No one can take these things away from you, and no one can belittle the woman who embraces these three truths. So put on your dancing shoes, girl, and laugh your way to victory!

# Just Get It Done

*A little extra sleep, a little more slumber,*
*and little folding of the hands to rest—then poverty*
*will pounce on you like a bandit; scarcity will attack*
*you like an armed robber.*

PROVERBS 24:33-34

You didn't want to get out of bed today. You wanted to stay safe and warm instead of facing all the challenges that were waiting for you outside in the world. But there are times when you just have to "get it done," no matter how you feel.

If there is something that you keep putting off, get it done today. It will not go away. It will not diminish. It will not just fade away. It will not dissipate with the morning dew. It will stand in defiance to your peaceful existence. It will destroy, tear down, disrupt, mutilate, and defy any good thing that enters your atmosphere. It will rob you of your sanity until you decide that you've had enough. It will only end when you do what you need to do and stand as a daughter of the King. So handle your business and get it done!

# Are You Growing?

*When I was a child, I spoke and thought and reasoned as*
*a child. But when I grew up, I put away childish things.*

1 CORINTHIANS 13:11

*Y*ou are growing. Changing. Each day brings wonder
that you've never seen before, and you're finally taking
the time to notice it. Wonderful surprises fill each moment.

It's time to laugh more, sing more, feel more, and love
more. It's time stop complaining and time to stop regretting.
Instead of wondering "What if?" and wallowing in the mud
of stagnancy, it's time to delight in life's treasures. This is the
day in which you will be filled with a passion for living like
no other time in your life. With each breath, it's time for you
to inhale a new fragrance. As you look into your life's mirror,
you will then see a new you. Sure, it's never easy to change,
but you can't grow if you stay where you are. So embrace
today to its fullest, and tomorrow you'll marvel at how far
you've come!

# Step into Your Miracles!

*For God is working in you, giving you the desire
and the power to do what pleases him.*

PHILIPPIANS 2:13

Today, decide to step into miracles. Today, choose to see the wonder of every moment. You are greater than you think and more awesome than you believe. Don't believe the lies that say you are unworthy! The amazing power that woke you up to behold another day has breathtaking opportunities set aside just for you. These opportunities have your name written on them! But you can't take hold of them if you don't recognize them and believe that they're yours for the taking! So today, choose to step into your miracles!

# Good Will Find You

*When you see these things, your heart will rejoice. You will flourish like grass! Everyone will see the LORD's hand of blessing on his servants.*

ISAIAH 66:14

*I*f you are unfriendly, you won't have friends. If you hang out with toxic people, you will become toxic yourself. And if you allow your atmosphere to become saturated with negative whispers, you will become negative. Negative energy is poisonous and impacts how you view life; how you treat others, and ultimately your quality of life. If you want to live an empowered life, be friendly. Don't deal in negative whispers and be a blessing to others. If you avoid all these things, you won't have to look for good. Good will find you.

# Dream Big!

*"You don't have enough faith," Jesus told them. "I tell you the truth, if you had faith even as small as a mustard seed, you could say to this mountain, 'Move from here to there,' and it would move. Nothing would be impossible."*

MATTHEW 17:20

When you dream big, everything changes. Your dream spills over into the atmosphere and then begins to attract big opportunities. Today your dream is coming true, and it's changing everything it touches. So dream big. Think big. Live big. Then allow your inner fire to burn through the obstacles and spread to every part of your life. Everyone who comes into contact with you will know that there is a different kind of light inside you. You're a woman who knows what she really wants and knows how to make her vision a reality!

# Value

*The Kingdom of Heaven is like a merchant on the lookout*
*for choice pearls. When he discovered a pearl of great value,*
*he sold everything he owned and bought it!*

MATTHEW 13:45-46

What do you value? Some women put value on accomplishment and the rewards that come with it. Others value hard work, money, or material goods. Maybe you value land or your home. Maybe you place the greatest value on a loving family.

There is nothing that makes you feel valuable like knowing that you are significant to others—knowing that you are touching and changing lives for good. You long to know your words, time, and energy are not being tossed aside like a dirty rag. Today, know that you have value! God made you and named you and gave His Son up for you. How's that for significant?

Know that someone is longing for you and what you bring. Value what you have and value who you are. Value that magnificent woman called you.

# Shout!

*May your priests be clothed in godliness;*
*may your loyal servants sing for joy.*

PSALM 132:9

There are times when you just have to shout! Shout because great opportunities call you by name. Shout because you can behold another day. Shout because you have the power to love someone. Shout because you can see joy all around you. Shout because you see the impossible become possible.

Shout when you hold the nervous, feed the hungry, and wipe the tears of the weary. Shout when you comfort the mourning, sit with the waiting, and support the weak. Shout the name of the One who is really at work! Shout when you see God snatch someone from the clutches of darkness. Shout when He lifts the cloud of depression. Shout when He helps someone stand in the midst of their trials. Shout when you see all that He does to help His children embrace their destiny!

# Hold Out

*An inheritance obtained too early in life
is not a blessing in the end.*

PROVERBS 20:21

Thinking of settling today? Maybe you just want a project to be finished, and instead of making it the best it can be you're ready to call it "good enough." Maybe a dream is in your reach, but it would take too much work to grasp it. You'll be content with what you have instead—even if it's not what you'd hoped or intended.

Don't settle. Hold out for what you want, you will never be disappointed. Don't settle for the mediocre when God is waiting to give you blessings beyond what you can imagine. So instead of holding on to the inferior, hold out for His best!

# Influence

*So be strong and courageous! Do not be afraid and do not panic before them. For the LORD your God will personally go ahead of you. He will neither fail you nor abandon you.*

DEUTERONOMY 31:6

*A* leader's influence is measured by the lives she touches for good. A leader chooses to respond when greatness calls her name. She chooses to stand when others fall. She chooses to fight when others surrender. She chooses to sacrifice when others hoard. She embraces her personal power and stands to face the impossible without apology. She understands that although it appears she is alone in their quest, a host of unseen others stand with her.

Today, choose to sit at tables where you can contribute without conflict or excessive competition. Where excessive competition thrives, progress cannot attend. Walk in paths where you understand the mission, where you can see the terrain, where you understand the terms of negotiation and you can share with like-minded leaders who share your fire. Then influence and lead without apology!

# Shadows

*I will lead blind Israel down a new path, guiding them along an unfamiliar way. I will brighten the darkness before them and smooth out the road ahead of them. Yes, I will indeed do these things; I will not forsake them.*

ISAIAH 42:16

Things might look bleak when you're standing in the shadows, but be encouraged! You can still see the sunlight. If it's cloudy in your world, know that there is bright sunlight waiting just above you. If you stand in sorrow's rain, you can still see the promise of a rainbow.

God has promised you that rainbow. Take hold of that promise! Nothing negative will last unless you embrace it and choose to dwell in it. Look for the ray of hope, the sparkle of light. It is always there if you look carefully, no matter how fiercely the storm rages or how gloomy the shadows may be.

# Love

*Three things will last forever—faith, hope, and love—
and the greatest of these is love.*

1 CORINTHIANS 13:13

*Three things will last forever...and the greatest of these is
love.* When life falls apart, Love glues it back together.
When you fall, Love lifts you to safety. When you feel lost,
Love shines and transforms darkness into day. When you
feel alone, Love holds you in His embrace. When you feel
like giving up, Love lifts your head and helps you to stand.
When you've lost your way on life's journey, Love shows you
another way of doing things, another way to live, another
way to breathe, another way to survive. When you collapse
in the arms of defeat, Love snatches you from his clutches,
lifts you up, breathes life into your dead dreams, and gives
you wings to fly. Turn to Love today.

# To Be Human

*O Lord, you have examined my heart and
know everything about me.*

PSALM 139:1

So many responsibilities are crowding each other out today, shouting for your attention. It's enough to make you want to cover your ears and run! "Hey!" you want to shout. "I'm not Superwoman! I can't handle all of this! I'm only human, you know!"

To be human is to be vulnerable. To be human is to know that you need others. To be human is to be open and transparent; to have needs and be able to express them. When you feel overwhelmed today, let yourself be human! Open yourself up to a friend and don't be afraid to ask for help. The successful woman knows that she didn't get where she is on her own!

# Reflecting

*And I am convinced that nothing can ever separate
us from God's love. Neither death nor life, neither angels
nor demons, neither our fears for today nor our worries
about tomorrow—not even the powers of hell can
separate us from God's love.*

ROMANS 8:38

It's the end of the day, and you lie in bed wondering what you should have done differently. You reflect on your choices, kicking yourself for the decisions you didn't make and the harsh words you spoke to a friend. You worry about tomorrow and the new challenges it will bring.

Tonight, realize that you cannot change what did or did not happen today, but look forward to things that hold promise in the coming season. Resolve to live more on purpose, love harder without fear, tolerate mediocrity less, empower those you love, and do things you've only dreamt of doing in newer, more interesting, and more fulfilling ways. No more procrastination. No more hesitation. No more excuses. Only movement. Only promise. Only hope. Only movement. Tomorrow's another day—and God will meet you there!

# Honor Others

*And may the LORD make us keep our promises to
each other, for he has witnessed them.*

1 SAMUEL 20:23

Honor others. Don't promise what you cannot deliver.
Don't say what you don't mean. You are known by
your word. If you keep it, then your image, your reputation,
is one of honor.

If you don't honor or keep your word, then you infect
the atmosphere with dishonor, surrounding yourself with a
foul stench. You cannot hide it because it follows you. You
can only change it by changing your behavior.

Always use sweet words because you may have to eat
them later. Either way, you will not forget the taste once you
eat them. Put pure action behind your words. There is nothing
more honorable than a woman who does what she says
she is going to do, when she said she would do it. Embrace
those who speak life, give life, and serve others. These are
women who understand the weight of their words, and
know that the promises they make matter for eternity.

# Impact

*And after the earthquake there was a fire,*
*but the LORD was not in the fire. And after the fire*
*there was the sound of a gentle whisper.*

1 KINGS 19:12

Have you ever felt God step into your life and impact you in such a profound way that the stench of yesterday's pain was wiped away? That the chains of self-doubt were broken? He held up a mirror and you saw yourself from a new vantage point. He presented you with the cup of liberty and asked you to drink, leaving you without excuse not to follow your dreams. He took nothing for Himself. He expected nothing. Borrowed nothing. He left your bank account filled with hope, wonder, love, peace, confidence, and all the necessary funding for achieving success. He saw the greatness in you and turned pages of your life that had been left untouched by other readers. He stood and read aloud your story for all to hear.

Did you listen as He read? If not, then it's time to stop giving in to negative whispers and listen for the still, small voice that is singing your life song.

# Ready to Run

*So I run with purpose in every step.*
*I am not just shadowboxing.*

1 CORINTHIANS 9:26

When you pull on your running shoes, you're already seeing the finish line! You're not going for a stroll—you have a race to win! You're standing at the starting line, and you're not looking around at the scenery. You're focused. You're determined. You're ready to go!

This is no place for amateurs. You're only going to win this race if you run with purpose—if you keep your eye firmly set on the goal and refuse to compromise. So when you hear that starting gun, don't hesitate. Don't wait one minute. Take off and run—it's time for you to soar!

# Take the Bat

*But I have spared you for a purpose—to show my power
and to spread my fame throughout the earth.*

EXODUS 9:16

*Y*ou've waited long enough! It's your turn up to bat. It's
your turn to show them who you are and what you've
got. Keep your eyes on the ball and swing hard! You can't
miss because you are a woman of focus and power.

Hey girl, you have the bat! That makes you dangerous.
You are dangerous to any distractions, obstacles, and negative influences. Just take your bat and knock them out of the
ballpark. They did not purchase tickets to your game. You
can run with purpose and touch every base without tear-
ing up your pantyhose. It's your turn to slide…into destiny!

# Tornado

*They were just trying to intimidate us, imagining that they could discourage us and stop the work. So I continued the work with even greater determination.*

NEHEMIAH 6:9

A tornado destroys everything in its path. It stirs the atmosphere with its terrible winds and commands center stage wherever it goes. It cannot be stopped. Nothing is safe that stands in its path.

A woman with focus is like a tornado. She stirs the winds of change and commands them to follow her lead. Once they hear and obey, she directs them to clear her path. She destroys the obstacles of frustration, procrastination, envy, depression, and strife with the wind of her focus. She moves all negative influences from her path with the sheer force of her determination. Like the tornado, she is dangerous to anything that attempts to obstruct her vision to purpose and obscures her path to destiny. In this, she is queen!

# You Are the Arrow

*We can make our plans, but the LORD determines our steps.*

PROVERBS 16:9

You are an arrow in the hands of a Warrior. You are focused, determined. Once He lets you go, you follow the path He has laid for you without swerving to the right or left.

So, sister, which way are you going? What is your course? What is the mission you've been put on this earth to accomplish? Where is the Warrior aiming you? He's released you from His bow and pointed you toward the target. Will you turn from that path when the wind comes and nudges you off course? Will you settle for striking the ground, or will you head straight for that bull's-eye?

But remember—this isn't just any warrior! Even if you've lost course and it doesn't look like you're going to hit the target, this Warrior can put you back on the right path. He determines our steps.

# Around Every Corner

*Therefore, whenever we have the opportunity,*
*we should do good to everyone—especially*
*to those in the family of faith.*

GALATIANS 6:10

round every corner is an opportunity to be victor or victim. Around every corner is an opportunity to either influence a person's life for good or to infect a person or situation for evil. Around every corner is an opportunity to do something miraculous or mediocre, to stand and defend a cause greater than what you can see or mightier than what you can feel, to change the minds of the doubtful or to empower the spirits of the faithful. Around every corner is the opportunity to either shine in the power of your strength or to cower in the darkness of your fear.

There's a corner just ahead. What will you do when you reach it?

# Step

*You have made a wide path for my feet
to keep them from slipping.*

2 SAMUEL 22:37

Step into the undiscovered wonder of a new day. Step into the thrill of discovering your unique gifts and talents. Step into the excitement that comes with a new beginning. Step into the arena and conquer your fears. Step into a new pair of shoes and dance the way you want to dance.

Sure, the first step on a new journey is hard. How will you handle all the unknown challenges that are sure to come your way? But take that first step, and then the next one, and then the one after that—and before long you'll see that those steps led to your destiny!

# The Bended Knee

*Confess your sins to each other and pray for each other so that you may be healed. The earnest prayer of a righteous person has great power and produces wonderful results.*

JAMES 5:16

If you want to change your world, master the art of the bended knee. Doctors have known for years that you need to bend your knees to lift a heavy weight. When you bend your knees, you also activate enough power to lift the weight off any situation that tries to hold you back from your purpose and your destiny.

So get on your knees, girl! Go to the Father in prayer, and you won't believe where He'll take you. When you take the bended-knee position, you also gain enough reserve strength to help someone else achieve their dreams. When you "stop and stoop" to help others, then it is only a matter of time before you start to see God at work. Go ahead girl, bend those knees and start talking to God!

# Be a Fragrance

*Yes, you should rejoice, and I will share in your joy.*
PHILIPPIANS 2:18

Go ahead and spray! You've earned it! The sweet smell of success is all over you! Now, let's get down to some serious business. Let's talk about the real deal! You know it's time to share the wealth. You've got more than enough of that sweet-smelling, purpose-attracting, destiny-grabbing perfume! When you share, you know it always comes back. And girl, think about the variety of fragrances we can sample if we all share. So go ahead. Spray some of that goodness on your sisters so we all can smell good!

# Write It Down

*Now go and write down these words. Write them in a book. They will stand until the end of time as a witness.*

ISAIAH 30:8

Go ahead and write it down! Keep a journal! Every God-given word you write contains power. Every God-given promise you believe drives you forward to purpose. Every God-given dream holds the key to your destiny.

And what's that key? It is taking hold of belief instead of giving in to doubt. Doubt stops all truth. Doubt walks hand-in-hand with obstacles. Hey, girl, you can't overcome obstacles if you doubt! This is your time. Go ahead and write the vision so that you and every person who stands with you can see it. Keep a record of all the promises God has made to you, and write down the ways you're seeing them fulfilled. Then those who believed will stand in awe!

# Fire!

*This is why I remind you to fan into flames the spiritual
gift God gave you...For God has not given us a spirit of
fear and timidity, but of power, love, and self-discipline.*

2 Timothy 1:6-7

God didn't give us little gifts. His gifts are a flame, and we
each have a torch to hold. But not everyone can carry
the fire. Not everyone is willing. Not everyone will take a
chance on getting burned.

It takes an extraordinary woman to carry enough fire to
light the way for her and for others. But girl, you've got what
it takes to light up the world around you. You are a woman
of destiny and power. You bring that fire with you wherever
you go. Girl, it's time to burn it up!

# Wild Arrows

*The heartfelt counsel of a friend is as sweet
as perfume and incense.*

PROVERBS 27:9

Wild arrows are dangerous. They fly aimlessly and hit unintended targets. An expert archer always hits their intended target. They always go for the bull's-eye. An expert archer knows that practice and focus are assets they cannot do without.

If you want to become an expert, only allow those with steady bows to counsel you. Surround yourself with archers who understand the power of your arm and the strength of your bow—archers who can see your target and cheer you on to victory. These expert archers help to determine where your arrows fly and help to define the type of archer you will become.

# Touch the Sky

*For since the world began, no ear has heard
and no eye has seen a God like you, who works for
those who wait for him!*

ISAIAH 64:4

Do you want to touch the sky? Do you want to soar above heights not known to others? Then you must do something others are not willing to do! You cannot allow fear to stop you. You cannot allow unbelief to hold you. And you must not allow others who cannot see your fire to enter your airspace. With a little faith, courage, and the right company, you can do anything.

Faith moves the mountains. Courage moves the hills. And the view is not for everyone. Not everyone's lungs can handle your atmosphere's richness! It is only for those who are unafraid of heights and wanting to touch the moon!

# Fly

*A person standing alone can be attacked and defeated, but two can stand back-to-back and conquer. Three are even better, for a triple-braided cord is not easily broken.*

ECCLESIASTES 4:12

Who says you can't fly? Who says you can't soar above adversity? Who says women can't rise together to meet challenges? Flying is easy when you do it with one of your sisters, and you can soar with more power when you do it with other women. Hey girl, didn't you know that challenges diminish in the heat of the fire when women unite? Go ahead and take your sister's hand. Hold her heart. She breathes, eats, sleeps, works, plays, and loves just like you. She longs to join you on the next flight. Remember this…it doesn't take wings to fly. It just takes courage! Do you have the courage to join your sisters and fly to destiny? If so, go ahead and fly. The world is waiting for what you have inside.

# The Destiny Key

*No, despite all these things, overwhelming victory is ours through Christ, who loved us.*

ROMANS 8:37

There's a destiny out there waiting for you—a destiny that is yours and yours alone. And you hold the key! You can use it when you discover your identity and grasp your purpose. Once you grasp your purpose, you become a dangerous woman. You become dangerous to negative people, places, and things. Those influences can no longer hold you captive.

So go ahead and use your key. It opens doors of purpose and promise. It opens the door to new horizons and new adventures. It has your name on it, and no one else can carry it. No one else can unlock the doors to the destiny that is yours alone!

# Fighting

*"Look!" he said. "The people are united, and they all speak the same language. After this, nothing they set out to do will be impossible for them!"*

GENESIS 11:6

What good does fighting your sister do? You both want the same thing. You both want to win! So why not stop the battle and fight together, standing side by side as you face down the forces of darkness and negativity? You become a formidable opponent when you join arms with your sisters! Together, you're a force to be reckoned with.

Link up your arms with another woman warrior and you will see things you never dreamed possible. You will see mountains that once blocked your way fall into the sea. You will see your crooked paths made straight. When you're united together and operating as one, nothing you set out to do will be impossible for you! You will see purpose, walk in power, and step into destiny…together!

# Much Is Required

*When someone has been given much, much will be
required in return; and when someone has been entrusted
with much, even more will be required.*

LUKE 12:48

You've got your briefcase, cell phone, and everything
else you need for business. You are Superwoman, and
you have a super mission. You've done things your mother
only dreamed of doing!

It's hard not to lose to yourself in the process because
success feels so good! But remember, others are watching
you. Others want to be like you. You are the only role model
some of them have. So, take some time to sit, relax, and share
your wealth of experience with them. Lavishly drape them
with your knowledge. Generously coat them with your savvy.
Abundantly paint them with your expertise. But above all
else, hug them with your acceptance. Remember…you have
much, so much is required.

# Time

*Yet God has made everything beautiful for its own time.*
*He has planted eternity in the human heart,*
*but even so, people cannot see the whole scope of God's*
*work from beginning to end.*

ECCLESIASTES 3:11

Time is a precious gift. When was the last time you
savored it? When was the last time you lingered in it
like a warm bath? Took delight in it like a piece of chocolate?
Have you luxuriated in it like a little girl wiggling her toes in
the mud after a hard rain?

Well, my sister, it is time you did! This precious moment
is all we have. All the busyness in the world will not recapture the time you wasted on things that don't really matter.
Take the time today to stop and enjoy this gift! Take the time
to contemplate the way you see your Father at work. Take
the time to treasure the things that matter for eternity. This
is your time—use it!

# To Those Who Hate You

*But to you who are willing to listen, I say, love your enemies! Do good to those who hate you.*

LUKE 6:27

Hey girl, you finally arrived! Delight in the moment—you've earned it! You've scaled mountains of opposition, crossed rivers of disappointment, and endured struggle's harsh terrain.

Now that the rough part is over, remember this...treat even your enemies fairly. If you do things the right way, they will watch your back better than those you call friends. Speak to them with kindness. Pour love over them like a gentle rain. Drip the honey of acceptance over their wounds. You have the power to change those relationships for the better!

# The Wind in Your Hair

*So let's not get tired of doing what is good. At just the right
time we will reap a harvest of blessing if we don't give up.*

GALATIANS 6:9

With the wind in your hair and the power of determination, you can do this thing! Don't give up, girl—you're almost there!

It's like priming one of those old water pumps. You've got to build up the pressure. If you stop before the water flows, you have to start pumping all over again. And when you do, there is no guarantee that your promises will still be there. That's the way it is with dreams. You can't let up on the pressure. You must keep dreaming. You must keep running. You must keep searching. You must keep priming your pump until you hit the flow. Come on girl, push into it! Remember your purpose and step into your destiny!

# You've Got It

*Plant the good seeds of righteousness,
and you will harvest a crop of love.*

Hosea 10:12

You've got it and you know it. Everyone else knows it too. So how are you going to use that strength? How are you going to use your power? Will you show kindness, love, and mercy? Or will revenge be your main objective? What fruit will come from your strength? What seeds will you plant today? What lives will you touch?

You've been to the gym and built up those muscles. And muscles are great, but it's what you do with your strength that counts. Strength without compassion is weakness. As you flex those muscles today, remember that lives will be changed by the way you use your power. Today you could be the key to change in someone's life. So go ahead! Change a life, inspire a mind, and touch the whole world. The world is waiting for what you bring to the table.

# The Burning Bridge

*Starting a quarrel is like opening a floodgate,*
*so stop before a dispute breaks out.*

PROVERBS 17:14

Could you walk across a burning bridge without fear? Without anxiety? Without trepidation and doubt?

Of course not! So before you light a fire that cannot be quenched, make sure you have a way of retreat. Don't burn that bridge, girl! You don't want to be in the middle of a battle and discover that you've burned all the bridges you need to retreat. Before you light that fire, consider the cost. Can you afford to become a casualty of war? If not, put your matches away and sign a peace treaty. An unburned bridge is a gift and a blessing. Today, choose to keep your bridges intact!

# Wisdom's Way

*Getting wisdom is the wisest thing you can do! And whatever else you do, develop good judgment.*

PROVERBS 4:7

Life is tough, and you've got to be ready to fight! And the more bitter the battle, the sweeter the victory... right?

There's a better way to knock down obstacles and break through to victory. It's called *wisdom*. Wisdom will take you farther than any boxing match and help you avoid all-out war in the first place. Why get bruised and bloodied when you can have peace and understanding instead? Wisdom tells you to study, develop strategies, network, and have patience. With wisdom on your side, life doesn't have to be a battle. Instead, it will be a sweet journey you take with friends!

# Dance, Girl! Dance!

*You thrill me, LORD, with all you have done for me!*
*I sing for joy because of what you have done.*

PSALM 92:4

$\mathcal{P}$ut on your dancing shoes! You've got so much to celebrate! Your new horizons are gleaming. New adventures await you at every twirl. So it's time to learn some new steps. Make some new moves, shake off some old stuff, and take a new look around. You are in a new place with a new attitude. You've earned the privilege to move into a new realm. Your age, height, weight, and dress size don't matter. All that matters is that you've got your shoes, and you're ready to dance. Go on, girl…let them see you step!

# Wonderful You

*I pray that from his glorious, unlimited resources he will*
*empower you with inner strength through his Spirit.*

EPHESIANS 3:16

What makes others want to share your atmosphere?
It's the way you smile when you make eye contact.
It's the way you greet others and change a nightmare of a day
into an experience of joy. It's the way you never let a bad day
get you down, and the way you always share your strength
and determination with a sister in need. That's the reason
others stand in line to drink from your fountain. It's the
reason they can't help but love you. So go ahead and smile
your world-famous smile, and flood your world with your
unique beauty. Remember, it radiates the wonder of the
wonderful you!

# There Is Nothing Like Freedom

*For the Lord is the Spirit, and wherever the Spirit
of the Lord is, there is freedom.*

2 CORINTHIANS 3:17

Nothing tastes like freedom. Nothing smells like joy!
Nothing excites like an accomplishment completed.
Nothing feels like a victory dance! And today it's time to celebrate how far you've already come on your journey to destiny.
Take a minute to reflect on everything you've accomplished
in the past season of your life, and congratulate yourself on
the tasks you've completed and the obstacles you've overcome. So, go on…live a little! Put on your best dress and
twirl! And thank God for giving you the freedom to be com-
pletely you, to fulfill the glorious destiny He has for you in
the way that only you can!

# One of Those Days

*So do not throw away this confident trust in the Lord.*
*Remember the great reward it brings you!*
*Patient endurance is what you need now, so that you*
*will continue to do God's will. Then you will*
*receive all that he has promised.*

HEBREWS 10:35-36

*I*t looks like it's going to be one of those days. You know the kind of day that makes you feel like you're trudging uphill through six inches of mud?

But looks can be deceiving. So girl, don't despair. Do some leg stretches. Do some toe tapping and get to walking. If you look closely, you'll see that a red carpet lines your road. All that mud was just an illusion, and there are grand and glorious riches awaiting you. Things worth having sometimes come with obstacles that only you can climb. So what are you waiting for? Start walking!

# Control

*Without wise leadership, a nation falls;*
*there is safety in having many advisers.*

PROVERBS 11:14

Sure, you're in control. You make the decisions about your home, your checkbook, your work, and all the projects on your plate. You're the queen of your own kingdom, right?

But remember...every queen has advisors. Every empress has a council. Every captain has a crew. You need others to help you guard and govern your realm. Don't make the mistake of trying to control everything on your own! Take the advice of those who have gone before you. Ask them questions and take advantage of their wisdom! You might be in charge of your life, but that doesn't mean you have to run it alone.

# Throw Your Hat into the Ring

*But our bodies have many parts, and God has put
each part just where he wants it...In fact,
some parts of the body that seem weakest and least
important are actually the most necessary.*

1 CORINTHIANS 12:18,22

Have an idea but think it will be ignored?

Have an opinion but think it will be ridiculed?

Want to participate but feel unqualified?

Throw your hat into the ring, girl! It might not look like the ones that are already there, but show off your style! Show off another way of doing things—the way that's uniquely you. Don't stay silent when you're called to speak up! You've got an important part to play in every situation you find yourself in, so put yourself out there!

# Climbing Mountains

*These trials will show that your faith is genuine. It is being
tested as fire tests and purifies gold—though your faith
is far more precious than mere gold. So when your faith
remains strong through many trials, it will bring you
much praise and glory and honor on the day when Jesus
Christ is revealed to the whole world.*

1 PETER 1:7

*H*ey girl! Hold your head up! You've climbed bigger
mountains and crossed terrain more roughed-up
than this before. Sister, don't forget who you are! You have
the image of Christ inside you, and you are mightier than
any mountain and more powerful than the wind and rain
that beat against your door! You are a wonder woman…and
even wonder women get tested.

So hold your head high! You're going to make it through
this challenge, make it to the top of this mountain. And if
you see more mountains in the distance, you won't lose heart!
You'll just smile and run to meet them!

# Think on Things

*And now, dear brothers and sisters, one final thing. Fix
your thoughts on what is true, and honorable, and right,
and pure, and lovely, and admirable. Think about things
that are excellent and worthy of praise.*

PHILIPPIANS 4:8

Stretch...relax. Breathe in...breathe out. Sounds easy,
right? It is for a woman like you! Stress, anger, distraction,
and fear delight in coming to visit you. But when they
show up for one of their unexpected visits, you just ignore
the ringing doorbell. You leave them standing at the door.
Time for them to visit someone else! You're not going to
entertain any negative thoughts. Instead, you take a nice
long bubble bath or a warm shower while you think on good
things. You think on things that are honorable, right, pure,
and lovely! Think on all the wonders that make you that
woman of influence. Think on those things that make you
fabulously you!

# Waves

*The LORD is my light and my salvation—so why should
I be afraid? The LORD is my fortress, protecting me from
danger, so why should I tremble?*

PSALM 27:1

It's a fact of life...waves come. Storms that invade
your shores. You cannot stop them, so you have two
choices: you can either run for cover or learn to ride the
waves. When the waves hit, the only thing that matters is
how you respond.

It's how you view these thunderous water walls that
determine your destiny. Will you allow them to conquer
you? Or will you grab your board and paddle out to meet
those waves? Will you let them overpower you or will you
take the ride of your life?

# Gifts Are for Giving

*The generous will prosper; those who refresh others will themselves be refreshed.*

PROVERBS 11:25

Give yourself away. Others are starving because you have a storehouse of nourishment at your banquet table. Serve a feast when you speak a kind word. Fill their cups when you touch their hearts. There are people waiting for the feast at your table.

God's given you more than enough—what are you hoarding it for? There are thirsty people all around you and you have more water than you know what to do with. And here's the best part: When you give them a glass of water, *you're* the one who feels refreshed. So give it away, girl!

# It Feels Good to Win

*In your majesty, ride out to victory,*
*defending truth, humility, and justice. Go forth*
*to perform awe-inspiring deeds!*

PSALM 45:4

It feels good to win! The victory is always sweet when you fight a hard fight. You won the battle against anger, strife, fear, and rejection. You won against negative thoughts and habits, envy, self-pity, and gossip. That means that you won some of life's toughest battles and came out victorious. You took no prisoners. You left all hindering forces in a state of shock from which they shall never recover. They cannot return to torment you. You won the war and won the prize. Girl, it's time to celebrate!

# Masterpiece

*He chose to give birth to us by giving us his true word.*
*And we, out of all creation, became his prized possession.*

JAMES 1:18

A masterpiece is born in the mind and heart of a master. The master then sketches his vision. After he sketches, he meticulously selects the colors, the type of paint, and determines the size of the canvas for his work. He then works at a feverish pace to complete his work and bring his vision to life. And upon completion, he looks upon it with love. It brings the master great joy. It brings the master the sweet feeling of accomplishment that can last a lifetime.

Girl, you are a masterpiece! Look in the mirror and see the Master's joy!

# How Sharp Are You?

*Tune your ear to wisdom,*
*and concentrate on understanding.*

PROVERBS 2:2

Sister, you've got it! You are just one of those women who has the edge in networking, researching, and training, in both your personal and professional life. The reason? You keep your skills current and you keep up with the latest trends and news. You keep yourself spiritually sound, morally focused, and physically active. You're going to stay sharp instead of falling behind!

But here's the big question: Can you share your sharpness and help another sister survive on the edge?

# 20/20

*May the Lord lead your hearts into a full
understanding and expression of the love of God and
the patient endurance that comes from Christ.*

2 Thessalonians 3:5

You've got 20/20 vision, girl! But how will you use it? Will you use it to peer back at the old actions and habits that used to hold you captive? Or will you use it to focus forward on all the possibilities that surround you? Take a closer look at all those glorious details that make you *you!* God's given you the gift of clear vision, so don't let it get clouded by doubt and illusion. Take a look around and rejoice!

# Can You Help a Sister Out?

*No one lights a lamp and then hides it or puts it under
a basket. Instead, a lamp is placed on a stand, where its
light can be seen by all who enter the house.*

LUKE 11:33

Can you help a sister out today? You've got the light of
hope inside you—can you give her a glimmer to help
light her way? Can you spare a candle to flicker in her path?

You've been there too. You've encountered the twists and
turns in your path—the curves you can't see past. Share some
of that light and illuminate the curve ahead for her. Help her
out the way someone helped you when it was too dark to see.
Send some of that sunshine to your sister today!

# Colors

*Arise, Jerusalem! Let your light shine for all to see. For the glory of the LORD rises to shine on you.*

ISAIAH 60:1

Without light, there is no color. Do you bring the light with you wherever you go? Do you change the atmosphere of strife into an ever-flowing fountain of miraculous, delicious color? What colors do others experience when you come into their presence? The red of anger? The green of envy? The pink of laughter, bubbling up and spilling over?

You've got the light. Use it to make the world brighter for your sisters! Help them see the colors all around them in richer, deeper, *real*er shades. Share the light with them and help illuminate the beauty all around them!

# Crossing Over

*Therefore…let us strip off every weight that slows us down,*
*especially the sin that so easily trips us up. And let us run*
*with endurance the race God has set before us.*

HEBREWS 12:1

Let's celebrate! You crossed over defeat, jealousy, envy, pride, and deceit. You did not allow them to conquer you on your journey. When the waves splashed and tried to pull you under, you fought a good fight. You climbed upon the riverbank, dried yourself off, and marched on toward your goals. You can now stand at the finish line and wave your victory flag. So celebrate your crossing! Celebrate your victory! Celebrate your destiny!

# Do You Feel the Beat?

*He saved us, not because of the righteous things*
*we had done, but because of his mercy. He washed*
*away our sins, giving us a new birth and*
*new life through the Holy Spirit.*

TITUS 3:5

o you hear the music? Do you feel the beat? It's a
new kind of music with a new kind of beat. It's
new because you're the one who's changed. You've changed
the way you move, the way you walk, and the way you talk.
You've changed your style and your smile. The new you
doesn't care what others say, what others think, or what others do. The new you loves her enemies and doesn't hold their
prejudices against them. You just breathe and move with
your new music. You just live, and love, and dance to your
new beat. You just love the wonder of your new discovery.
You just love being…you!

# Like There's No Tomorrow

*In his kindness God called you to share in his eternal glory
by means of Christ Jesus. So after you have suffered a little
while, he will restore, support, and strengthen you, and he
will place you on a firm foundation.*

1 PETER 5:10

Who told you that you couldn't do a split? Who told you that you couldn't dance and jump at the same time? Who told you that age was a factor in your zeal for life, in your energy level, in your overall attitude, or in your feminine appeal?

Well, sister…it's time to dance like you are in your twenties. Jump like there is no tomorrow and reach for the highest star. And while you're dancing and reaching, remember this…you're better at reaching, and teaching, and dancing, and prancing, and loving, and living now than when you were in your twenties! Age has just made you better!

# Move

*See, I am sending an angel before you to protect*
*you on your journey and lead you safely to the*
*place I have prepared for you.*

EXODUS 23:20

You've been comfortable for a while now—and that's not a bad thing! But now it's time to get going. It's time to move to uncharted territory.

It's only uncharted because you haven't been there to claim it and to mark it and make it yours. It awaits your arrival, and it awaits your flag waving boldly on the shore. The sea of change is calling you. The winds now whisper your name. Take your boat and sail toward your horizon of purpose. Take your balloon and ride upon the winds to destiny. It's time to move into a new realm of peace and discovery... a new realm of being you.

# Friends

*Never abandon a friend.*
PROVERBS 27:10

There are people who just shake your hand and never let you get beyond the acquaintance stage. There are people who keep you at arm's length and never let you get too close. There are people who hug you but do not become intimate. But then there are the real friends—the people who embrace you, faults and all. They love you even on those days when you have bad hair and a worse attitude. They love and embrace you on your "wounded porcupine" days. They hold up the shield and take the quills of anger, whining, and unhappiness you send their way and when the quill shooting is over, they are still standing…still standing with you.

# Take a Journey

*Can two people walk together without*
*agreeing on the direction?*

AMOS 3:3

How can you take a journey with someone unless you both agree to go to the same place? How can you pack up the car for a road trip and start driving without having a destination in mind?

Two women who are walking together in agreement make up a powerful force. And walking doesn't mean just walking. It doesn't mean just talking. Walking means sharing trials, troubles, and the cost of the journey. So when you choose a partner, choose one who shares your destination! You need a sister who not only wants to travel, but a sister who can lift you when you're tired and inspire you when you want to give up. And when you find a sister like that, keep her close! Walk with her every step of the way.

# Better Than Money

*Dear friends, let us continue to love one another,*
*for love comes from God. Anyone who loves is a child*
*of God and knows God.*

1 JOHN 4:7

What's better than money, harder to come by, and easier to lose? What is more precious than gold, more costly than silver, and more fragile than glass? What brings smiles, causes pain, keeps you from falling, but gives truth when you want something else? What brings the comfort of a warm cup of coffee but irritates you like sandpaper?

It's something that lasts. It's something that sustains. It's something beautiful. It's something wondrous and marvelous. It's something that I don't want to live without. It's precious, costly, and fragile, brings smiles, creates joyous pain, brings truth, and gives comfort.

So what is the identity of this treasure? It's you and your friendship!

# You've Got Jewels

*Joyful are those who obey his laws and search
for him with all their hearts.*

PSALM 119:2

Jewels line your life. Can you see them? Can you see the radiance? Can you touch the shine? Can you feel their heat? Can you taste their colors? Can you hear their clarity? They are waiting for the chance to shine, for the chance to be noticed, for the opportunity to bring joy, clarity, radiance, and heat into your life. They belong to you. Someone marvelous put them there just for you.

Wear a ring of promise! Create a necklace of joy! Dance in pearls of laughter! Wear your earrings of gold and your anklet of silver! Deck yourself with these jewels and then shine, feel the heat, see the radiance, and taste the colors of your newfound identity. You are dripping in the jewels of purpose, so go ahead and walk in it girl!

# The Eyes Have It

*Once you had no identity as a people;*
*now you are God's people.*

1 PETER 2:10

For so long you've believed the lies the world says about you. You're inconvenient. You're unloved. You're unnecessary.

But today, listen to what your Father, the King, says about you! He says you are wonderful, and He says you have greatness in you! He says you are a woman of excellence, and He says that with His strength, you can do anything you decide to do. He says that you have power, strength, intelligence, wisdom, and endurance.

He's given you strength when you were weak. He's spoken life when death was all around you. He's stood by you in times of darkness, and when you couldn't see He's been your light. He says it. Believe it!

# Clouds

*If your gift is to encourage others, be encouraging. If it is
giving, give generously. If God has given you leadership
ability, take the responsibility seriously. And if you have a
gift for showing kindness to others, do it gladly.*

ROMANS 12:8

Clouds form as the heat from the sun evaporates water,
and then they burst and release their rain on the earth
below. Clouds are a critical part of the life cycle on this planet.
Without them, there would be no nourishing rain on the
earth.

A woman with purpose is like a cloud. She fills her life
with purposeful things by reading, learning, and being in
the company of purposeful people. She then empties herself
out and shares with other women. Like the clouds, she is a
critical part of the sisterly life cycle. She is ever forming, ever
bursting, ever nourishing others with showers of blessing.

# Trees

*They are like trees planted along a riverbank, with roots
that reach deep into the water. Such trees are not bothered
by the heat or worried by long months of drought. Their
leaves stay green, and they never stop producing fruit.*

JEREMIAH 17:8

A tree that's planted close to the water is full of fruit.
Its leaves are always green, and its roots grow down
deep. It's the best kind of tree for birds to build their nests in,
for children to climb in, and for people to seek shade under.

Are you like that tree? Do you bear good fruit? Do you
show life and vibrancy with every word you speak? Are your
roots growing deep down into the source of life? It takes a
mighty force to uproot a tree, but girl, you're planted deeply
in God. There's no force on earth that can uproot you and
take you away from that water!

# Hold the Wheel

*The LORD will work out his plans for my life—for
your faithful love, O LORD, endures forever.
Don't abandon me, for you made me.*

PSALM 138:8

It's time to begin a new phase of your life's journey, and you're holding the wheel! But girl, you can't drive forward looking in the rearview mirror! You only need it to glance back before you change lanes. If you focus on the past, you will miss your exit to destiny.

Today marks a new assignment for you. It's time to change lanes and take the exit marked with your name! Take the road designed and fashioned just for you. And as you take the exit to discover the next blessing God is bringing into your life, my most heartfelt wish for you is to arrive at your best destination. Arrive at the place where you will shine!

# Diamonds

*Always be joyful. Never stop praying.*
*Be thankful in all circumstances, for this is God's*
*will for you who belong to Christ Jesus.*

1 THESSALONIANS 5:16-18

It isn't easy to make a diamond. Those jewels are made up of ordinary chemicals that have been put under extraordinary pressure. Sure, the pressure's tough, but it's necessary if a piece of coal is ever going to turn into a precious gem.

You're like that diamond. You thrive under pressure. You shine when darkness tries to overtake your position. You are not a woman who is easily moved by life's circumstances or swayed by the opinions of others. You live in the light, and you know how to shine!

# Broken Arms

*Watch out for people who cause divisions and upset
people's faith by teaching things contrary to what you have
been taught. Stay away from them.*

ROMANS 16:17

Remember this: Two broken arms do not a victory make. Real strength and power sometimes comes from walking away. Don't let anyone cause you to lose your cool or waste your energy. Sister, you've got more important things to do than fight unneccesary wars. The woman you are fighting may be the best warrior to walk side by side with you into a battle that really matters. So count the cost of the war and see if you can afford to pay it. Your sister may be just who you need to defeat your real enemy—division. It takes a person of real strength to move the mountain of pride. It takes a woman of real power to extend her arm and bridge the gap of anger and division.

# Hiding Is Not an Option

*God rescued me from the grave, and now
my life is filled with light.*

JOB 33:28

When an ostrich is afraid, it panics and digs its head into the sand. It thinks that because it can't see the danger, it no longer exists.

Have you tried to hide your head in the sand? It doesn't work any better for you than it does for the ostrich. You can't hide from life! And why would you ever try? You have an inner light that is so bright that it blinds your adversaries. You have an inner strength that confuses those who try to tear you down with false words. But you also have a softness that reminds others that you are uniquely female, uniquely beautiful, and uniquely wonderful. Remember, there is no one like you. Next time you hear the roaring lions and try to duck and cover, stand up. Face them. Be bold. Shine your light!

# Flowing Ideas

*Oh, don't worry; we wouldn't dare say that we are as
wonderful as these other men who tell you how important
they are! But they are only comparing themselves with
each other, using themselves as a standard of measurement.
How ignorant!*

2 Corinthians 10:12

Competition. Comparison. Corruption. These three
habits are toxic, sticking a knife into cooperation,
teamwork, companionship, and mutual growth. But you
won't let the Toxic Cs bring you down! You are a bright light
that shines in darkness! When others cannot see, you bring
a smile. When others are unkind, you speak words of light
and life. When you're around, the Toxic Cs disappear. You
get rid of competition because you know who you are and
refuse to compete. You dash comparison on the rocks of self-
assurance. You take corruption and kick it out of your path.

Now it's time to reach out and help others see their own
inner lights. Touch others with your light and watch as your
dreams overtake you!

# Lift Up Your Hands

*Lift up holy hands in prayer, and praise the LORD.*
PSALM 134:2

Lift up those hands, girl! Just think of all the things that can happen when you do. When you lift your hands, you can hail a cab or stop someone from advancing. Lifting your hands lets others know that you've had enough or that you have something to say. And it's one way for you to bring praise to the Father!

Today, get those hands up in the air! Worship the Lord and glorify Him! When you see Him at work, lift up your hands and sing a song of praise!

# The Power of Womanhood

*She gets up before dawn to prepare breakfast for her household and plan the day's work for her servant girls.*

PROVERBS 31:15

Who says you can't balance life and a career? Whoever said it must not know the true strength and power of womanhood. You can manage it, because you know how to give your energy and attention to the task right in front of you. You work hard, but you know how to play hard too! And most important of all, you know how to ask for help when you really need it. You know you can't do it all without your sisters!

You've got one arm for work and the other for play. One hand for wiping up a mess and the other for scheduling that meeting. Multitasking is your middle name—but you know that real joy comes from *connection!*

# Stargazer

*For ever since the world was created, people have
seen the earth and sky. Through everything God made,
they can clearly see his invisible qualities—
his eternal power and divine nature. So they have
no excuse for not knowing God.*

ROMANS 1:20

When's the last time you went out at night to look
up at the stars? Did you lean your head back and
gaze in wonder at the lights twinkling above you? Stars
remind us that there is a power so much greater than our-
selves. They remind us that we are not alone in the universe.
They stand as a testament to love and the awesome power of
our Creator God.

Take some time to go stargazing today. Take the time to
notice the miracles you usually overlook. Look for the ways
God's showing Himself to you! Go ahead girl! The stars are
calling your name!

# Put on Your Armor

*Put on all of God's armor so that you will be able to stand firm against all strategies of the devil.*

EPHESIANS 6:11

Put on your armor, girl! Put on your helmet because a girl can always use a good hat that shields her ears from gossip. It blocks darts sent just to give her a headache. Put on your breastplate because it covers your heart and blocks arrows sent to wound you. Put on your belt of truth because a girl can always use another good accessory, especially one that has a purpose! Put on your boots because they are made for walking and they help you escape danger. Hold up your shield because it will faithfully block the bullets of jealousy, envy, and strife. And above all else, remember to bring your sword. Girl, it's rough out there so you've got to protect yourself! So before you face the world, remember to put on your armor!

# When All Is Said and Done

*I have fought the good fight, I have finished the race, and
I have remained faithful.*

2 TIMOTHY 4:7

hen you come to the end of your life, you want
it said that you gave unselfishly, loved passion-
ately, fought valiantly, stood firmly, lived righteously, and
walked fearlessly. At that moment there will be no more fear,
doubt, insincerity, deceit, or toxic whispers. There will only
be rejoicing in the heroic life you lived!

We all want to be remembered as world-changers. What
can you do today to build that legacy?

# Stay Plugged In

*For the LORD God is our sun and our shield. He gives us*
*grace and glory. The LORD will withhold no good thing*
*from those who do what is right.*

PSALM 84:11

~

*Y*ou stay plugged into the source! You understand that
you cannot live out your destiny without the power
of the Holy Spirit! You understand that nothing will ever
be accomplished if you're not plugged in to His power. His
power is ever-present, ever-giving, and ever-flowing. His
Power created the moon and stars, so He doesn't have any
problem providing light for the night portion of your journey. His Power created the oceans, so you should have no
fear of crossing rivers. His Power created the mountains, so
you should have no fear of hills. He has given you the voice
to speak so that the mountains will move and block your
path no more!

So stay plugged into the Power source. There is nothing
like feeling the Spirit flowing through you and showing others the awesome presence of His marvelous light!

# Unless

*Put on your new nature, and be renewed as you learn to know your Creator and become like him.*

COLOSSIANS 3:10

nless you step into the arena, there will be no victory. Unless you become vulnerable, you cannot give or receive love. Unless you accept your greatness, there will be no mountains for you to move. Unless you arm yourself for war, there will be no battles won. Unless you share your gifts with others, you cannot grow together. Unless you run a race, you will never know how fast and how far you can run. Unless you pick up a bow, you will never know how to sharpen your aim and hit your mark. Unless you speak up for righteousness, you will never know the strength of winning a good moral fight.

Girl, you are a

**D**etermined

**I**nnovative

**V**ictorious

**A**chiever!

So step into the arena and speak up for righteousness!

# Successful Ingredients

*You see, his faith and his actions worked together. His actions made his faith complete.*

JAMES 2:22

Have you ever wondered why some people succeed and others don't? Is it a sheer force of will? Strong character? A lot of good luck?

Success means a lot of hard work. It's not going to be dumped in your lap! But hard work will get you noticed. Hard work will connect you with others—people who can bring you golden opportunities and resources. Hard work comes about because of a burning passion and a drive to succeed. Without that drive, who would ever do the hard work of overcoming obstacles?

Do you have that drive? Are you willing to put in the work? Then girl, keep at it! Success is on its way!

# Letting Go

*While we live in these earthly bodies, we groan and sigh,*
*but it's not that we want to die and get rid of these bodies*
*that clothe us. Rather, we want to put on our new bodies*
*so that these dying bodies will be swallowed up by life.*

2 CORINTHIANS 5:4

Letting go doesn't mean giving in to despair or destruction. When you let go of anger, you give in to joy. When you let go of fear, you give in to freedom. When you let go of gossip, you give in to positive connections and powerful words. When you let go of jealousy and gossip, you give in to acceptance and celebration. When you let go of hate, you give in to love and new relationships.

It's time to let go and give in and watch your life explode with abundant joy!

# Paint Your World

*For you have been born again, but not to a life that will
quickly end. Your new life will last forever because it
comes from the eternal, living word of God.*

1 PETER 1:23

Is it time to change the color scheme of your life? If so,
don't hand someone else the paintbrush! Girl, you've
got to get out the paintbrush and choose your own colors.
Unleash your artistic flair. Allow the colors of your dreams to
permeate the fabric of your purpose. Ride upon the wind of
your creativity. Paint your life with self-acceptance, determination, focus, and the desire to walk in your destiny.

These colors are not easily found in any home improve-
ment store. One can only special order the paint from heavenly hardware stores. Drape your life with joy and you will
become empowered to live your dreams…in living color!

# But a Vapor

*For the things we see now will soon be gone, but the
things we cannot see will last forever.*

2 CORINTHIANS 4:18

Some people prefer silver and gold over relationships.
Some people prefer houses, land, or material wealth
over connecting with others. Some people prefer the company of those rich in money and poor in character. They do
all they can do to attract and keep their corrupt companionship and stay connected to things made valuable by man.

What does your heart long for? Who shares your company? Who do you sit with, sup with, laugh with, and stand
with? Where do you expend the real riches of your life?
Remember, our words and actions will echo throughout
eternity. When we touch a life for good, it's not just a fleeting connection. Are you working for eternity today?

# Finish

*And I am certain that God, who began a good work*
*within you, will continue his work until it is finally*
*finished on the day when Christ Jesus returns.*

PHILIPPIANS 1:6

Finish what you start, our mothers said. Finish your work. Finish your sentences. Finish your plans.

That's still good advice. Finish doing what is right. Finish your race. Finish your assignment. Finish telling your life story to your children. Finish the work you are given and victory will be the end result.

Girl, you're going to be victorious today! You finish what you start, so you can go out in victory!

Gail M. Hayes has served as a consultant to women in the workplace by helping them to improve their relationships and become agents of change. Because of her passion for helping working women (whether they are working on an assembly line, making power decisions from the board room, or standing at a diaper-changing table), she developed the Handle Your Business Girl Empowerment Network, empowering women who want to make connections with other women.

To learn more about books by Gail M. Hayes
or to read sample chapters,
log on to our website:
**www.harvesthousepublishers.com**

# Successful Women Think Differently
### *9 Habits to Make You Happier, Healthier, and More Resilient*

By Valorie Burton

Popular author and professional certified coach Valorie Burton knows that successful women think differently. They make decisions differently. They set goals differently and bounce back from failure differently. Valorie is dedicated to help women create new thought processes that empower them to succeed in their relationships, finances, work, health, and spiritual life. With new, godly habits, women will discover how to:

- focus on solutions, not problems
- choose courage over fear
- nurture intentional relationships
- take consistent action in the direction of their dreams
- build the muscle of self-control

In this powerful and practical guide, Valorie provides a woman with insight into who she really is and gives her the tools, knowledge, and understanding to succeed.

# 7 Seconds to Success
*How to Effectively Relate to People in an Instant*

### By Gary Coffey & Bob Phillips

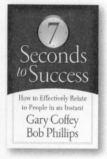

Success depends on making a great impression and effectively relating to people. Those first few seconds with someone can make all the difference. Bestselling author Bob Phillips and leadership expert Gary Coffey have distilled the essential skills of reading and understanding people into easy-to-remember principles. Readers will discover the best ways to relate to and connect with individuals, including how to:

- identify the best approaches to create good will
- know how to communicate with all personality types
- spark and keep people's interest

*7 Seconds to Success* provides the tools necessary to improve people skills and garner trust. Every interaction can be positive and rewarding!

# God's Unlikely Path to Success
*How He Uses Less-Than-Perfect People*

By Tony Evans

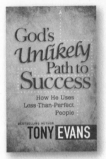

When many Christian readers think of the heroes of the Bible, they think about how "good" they were. They forget that…

- Rahab was a harlot.
- Jonah was a rebel.
- Moses was a murderer.
- Sarah was a doubter.
- Peter was an apostate.
- Esther was a diva.
- Samson was a player.
- Jacob was a deceiver.

And yet these eight men and women are among the Bible's greatest heroes.

Dr. Tony Evans uses these prominent Bible characters to illustrate the truth that God delights in using imperfect people who have failed, sinned, or just plain blew it. These are men and women whose actions—or reactions—were not consistent with God's character—and yet God met them and used them in the midst of their mess.

Readers will be encouraged about their own walk with God as they come to understand that He has them, too, on a path to success, *despite* their many imperfections and mistakes.